3-D THRILLERS!

SNAKES
and Other Extraordinary Reptiles

SAMANTHA HILTON

■Scholastic

New York • Toronto • London • Auckland
Sydney • Mexico City • New Delhi • Hong Kong

SNAKES ALIVE!

Snakes are part of the reptile family. This also includes crocodiles, lizards, and turtles. But snakes are more than just legless lizards. These amazing animals can burrow, climb trees, and swim, and some can even glide through the air!

▼ Snake babies

From the moment they hatch from their eggs, most snakes have to take care of themselves. The female snake lays a number of soft, leathery eggs in a hole in the ground or in a big pile of rotting vegetation. A baby snake breaks out of its egg using a special egg tooth, which it loses after it hatches. Not all snakes lay eggs. A female rattlesnake carries her eggs inside her body and gives birth to live young. After a few days with their mother, these young snakes face the world alone.

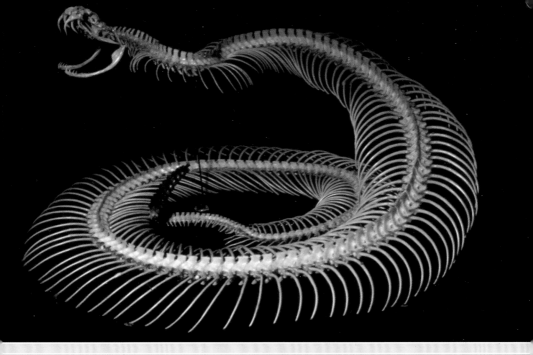

▲ Bony bodies

All snakes have bony skeletons and backbones. Amazingly, snakes have more than 110 bones, or vertebrae, along their backbones, compared to only 24 in humans. They also have about the same number of ribs running down the length of their backbones.

Sun-loving snakes ▶

Like all reptiles, snakes are cold-blooded. This means they cannot generate their own body heat. Snakes use the warmth of their surroundings to get their bodies moving. Sometimes they can be spotted warming themselves in the morning sun. If snakes get too cold, they become slow and sluggish. For this reason, most snakes are found in the warmer parts of the world.

Some snakes are VENOMOUS. This means they inject poison into their PREY when they bite them!

SLITHERING

M any people are truly terrified of snakes, even though they may never have seen one in person. Most snakes are shy and harmless. Even venomous snakes will bite you only if they are provoked or surprised.

A snake's SKIN may look wet and slimy, but it is actually dry and covered in SCALES.

▼ Fang-tastic

When a rattlesnake prepares to attack, its fangs unfold from the roof of its mouth. Just before it strikes, its fangs become fully erect at the outer edge of the upper jaw. A rattlesnake's fangs are sharp and hollow. They are perfect for injecting poison into prey.

SERPENTS

◄ Hooded King

The king cobra is the world's deadliest venomous snake. It can deliver enough venom in a single bite to kill an elephant. The king cobra is also the largest type of cobra. It can reach 18 feet (5.5 m) in length.

Open wide! ►

Snakes' teeth all point backward into their mouths because snakes swallow their food whole. Although snakes can hold on to their prey, they can't chew it up. Instead, they have very flexible jaws. They open their mouths as wide as possible and swallow prey in one piece, usually headfirst. That way, the prey's limbs, fur, or feathers lie flat against its body, and it slides down the snake's throat more easily! A snake's skin and stomach are stretchy enough to allow it to eat large animals.

SUPER SNAKE

Snakes are predators, which means they have to catch and eat other animals in order to survive. They use their sharp senses to hunt, escape danger, and find mates. Some snakes have poor vision, so they use their other senses to make up for their bad eyesight.

▼ Sixth sense

Most animals have five senses—sight, hearing, touch, taste, and smell. However, some snakes, such as rattlesnakes and vipers, have another sense: They can sense heat. These snakes have pits on the front of their faces that can detect small changes in temperature. This is very useful when hunting at night. Mammals give off heat from their bodies, and the snake senses this small rise in temperature. Then it locates its mammalian prey and moves in for the kill!

SENSES

BLIND SNAKES spend most of their lives BURROWING underground. They can tell light from dark, but not much else.

◀ Smelly tongue

Although snakes have nostrils, they actually smell with their tongues. When a snake sticks out its tongue, it is smelling its surroundings. The moist tongue detects smells from the air and the ground. A snake has a notch in its upper jaw that it can stick its tongue through without even opening its mouth.

Ear, ear ▶

If you look closely at a snake—not too closely, though!—you'll see that it has no ears. Instead, snakes "hear" by sensing vibrations through the ground. In this way, a snake can tell if prey or a predator is coming. Some snakes also use camouflage to hide from predators. The skin of these snakes is similar in color to their surroundings.

SNAKES ON

You'd think that having no legs would be a real problem—but not for a snake! Snakes have many vertebrae, which make their backbones very flexible. These reptiles have devised lots of amazing ways of getting around.

▼ Burrowing beast

The horned viper lives in the sweltering Sahara Desert in Africa. Like all snakes, the viper is a meat eater. It feeds on lizards, mammals, and birds. The viper will often bury itself in the sand using rapid sideways movements of its body; then it lies waiting with only its horns and eyes exposed. When it senses its prey nearby, it explodes from the sand and strikes its victim with lightning speed.

THE MOVE

◀ Falling with style

"Flying snakes" can't really fly—they glide or free-fall from tree to tree. To prepare for takeoff, a flying snake slithers onto the end of a high tree branch. Then it pushes itself off the branch using the lower half of its body. It flattens its body to twice its normal width so it can catch the air and glide. By twisting its body in the air, this amazing snake can even make turns in order to land where it wants.

Sidewinder ▶

Snakes move in different ways, depending on the surface they are on. The sidewinder snake gets its name from the curious sideways motion it makes. Gripping hot, sliding sand is difficult. So sidewinders, like other desert snakes, throw their bodies forward instead of slithering along the ground.

MIND YOUR

Biting your enemies, spitting in their eyes, and sticking out your tongue are not considered good manners. But in the snake world, this is pretty normal behavior!

▼ Close your eyes!

Spitting may be a gross habit, but it's a great form of defense! The spitting cobra can send a stream of venom from its mouth directly into the eyes of anything it feels to be a threat. The poison causes a burning sensation in the victim's eyes and warns off any potential predators.

▲ Talented tongue

A snake's tongue is forked, which helps the snake smell very effectively. When the tongue flicks back into the snake's mouth, it touches something called the Jacobson's organ. This tells the snake what it is smelling. The tips of the tongue fit into the two openings to this organ. If the smell is stronger on one side than the other, the snake will know that the smell is coming from this direction.

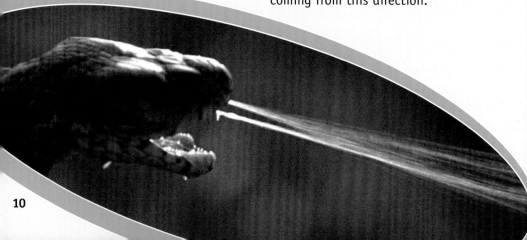

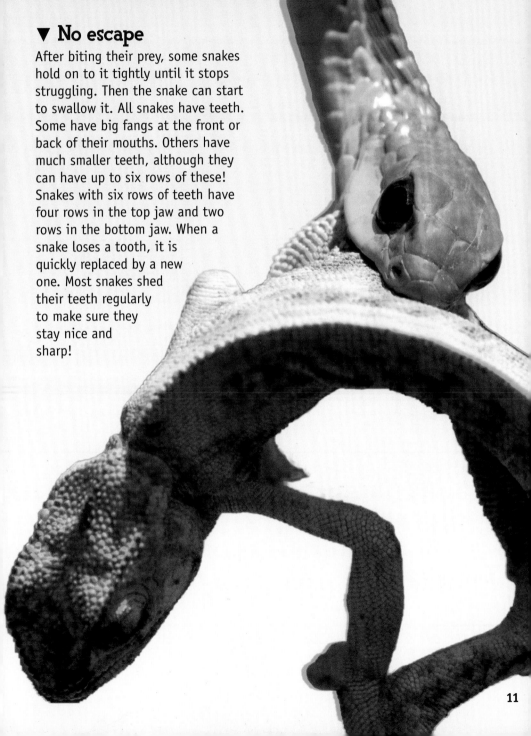

MANNERS!

▼ No escape

After biting their prey, some snakes hold on to it tightly until it stops struggling. Then the snake can start to swallow it. All snakes have teeth. Some have big fangs at the front or back of their mouths. Others have much smaller teeth, although they can have up to six rows of these! Snakes with six rows of teeth have four rows in the top jaw and two rows in the bottom jaw. When a snake loses a tooth, it is quickly replaced by a new one. Most snakes shed their teeth regularly to make sure they stay nice and sharp!

PUTTING THE

Not all snakes rely on biting and poisoning to catch prey. Pythons, anacondas, and boas are constrictors. A constrictor winds its body around its prey and squeezes until the victim suffocates and dies.

It can take several weeks for a CONSTRICTOR to DIGEST a large meal, such as a deer.

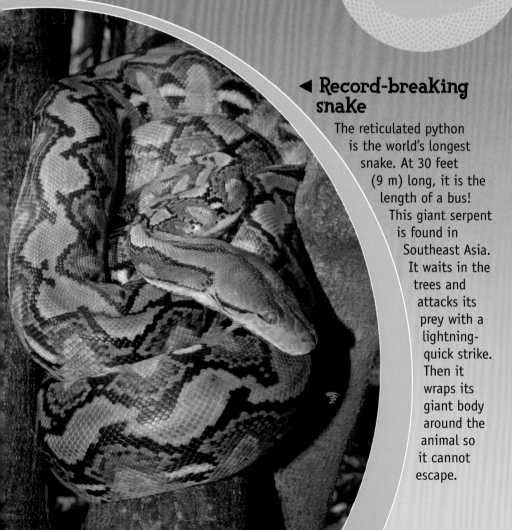

◀ Record-breaking snake

The reticulated python is the world's longest snake. At 30 feet (9 m) long, it is the length of a bus! This giant serpent is found in Southeast Asia. It waits in the trees and attacks its prey with a lightning-quick strike. Then it wraps its giant body around the animal so it cannot escape.

SQUEEZE ON

Beware of the boa ▶

Boa constrictors live in tropical Central and South America. They will eat almost anything, from mice, birds, frogs, and lizards to monkeys and pigs. The size of a boa's prey increases as the snake grows older and larger.

◀ Heavyweight

Anacondas spend a lot of time in shallow water, hidden from prey. They may not be as long as their python relatives, but they are certainly heavier. They can weigh more than 550 pounds (249 kg)—as much as three grown men! This giant snake can open its mouth wide enough to swallow large prey, such as jaguars and caimans. It does this by unhinging its lower jaw, which is connected to the upper jaw by stretchy ligaments. Then it slowly swallows the animal whole!

YOU HAVE BEEN

Despite their fearsome reputation, most snakes don't go looking for trouble. They tend to bite only when people step on them by accident. Snakes usually prefer flight to fight, and will go to great lengths to warn or scare animals and people away!

Big head! ▶

One way of scaring off predators is to make yourself look bigger than you are. A cobra has a flap of skin, called a hood, behind its head. This can be expanded outward when the snake is about to strike. When it is threatened, the cobra raises its head and upper body, shows its fangs, and hisses loudly.

WARNED!

Hognose snakes pretend to be dead to keep PREDATORS from eating them!

Shake, rattle, and roll ▶

The end of a rattlesnake's tail is made up of sections of loosely linked bony material. If the snake is threatened, it shakes its tail as a warning. The harsh, buzzy sound is enough to scare many animals and people away.

▼ Color code

Many animals use bright colors as a warning device, and snakes are no exception. This coral snake's brightly colored skin warns its enemies that it is poisonous. This clever defense is copied by some nonpoisonous snakes as well. Milk snakes look like coral snakes to make predators think they are deadly.

MAN BITES

Some people's fear of snakes means they kill them for no good reason. In fact, snakes are very useful. Many feed on rats, which keeps the rodent population down. Some species make good pets. Snake venom can also be used to treat illnesses such as stroke, cancer, and heart problems.

▼ Snake cure

Venom is sometimes used in modern medicine. It is extracted from snakes by a harmless process known as milking. The snake's fangs are pressed against a jar, which causes the venom to seep out. Venom is also used to make antivenom. If you are unlucky enough to be bitten by a snake, you will be given an antivenom to help you recover.   In some parts of Asia, many snakes are killed for use as ingredients in traditional medicine.

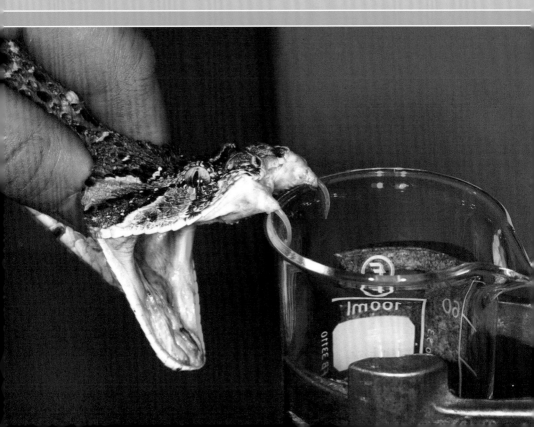

SNAKE

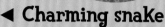
Snakes are often killed for their SKIN. It is used to make bags, belts, jewelry, and shoes.

◄ Charming snake

For centuries, snake charmers in India have used cobras to entertain crowds. Although the charmer appears to use music to charm the snake, the animal is actually responding to his movements. The charmer taps his foot and sways, and the snake moves in time with the vibrations.

Snaky pets ►

Snakes are fascinating creatures, and with regular handling they can become somewhat tame. Some species, such as milk snakes and corn snakes, make excellent pets. Snakes don't shed pet hair all over the house, you don't need to take them out for walks, and they are very quiet. However, you do need to feed them live food, such as mice and rats, from time to time!

ALL KINDS OF

Snakes and lizards are probably the best-known members of the reptile family. The group also includes turtles, crocodiles, and chameleons. Reptiles can be found all over the world, except in Antarctica and the coldest oceans.

Meet the ancestors ▶

Dinosaurs were reptiles, too. They were possibly cold-blooded and laid eggs. But most of them had longer legs and could cover more ground than reptiles today can. So the next time a snake scares you, be grateful it isn't a *T. rex* instead!

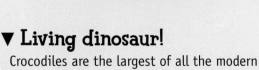

▼ Living dinosaur!

Crocodiles are the largest of all the modern reptiles and are similar to their ancient cousins, the dinosaurs. They have heavily armored skin and bone-crushing jaws. Crocodiles are excellent swimmers, and they can overpower most prey— from large fish to deer.

REPTILES

Not a pretty sight! ▼

The marine iguana of the Galápagos Islands is an odd-looking reptile. Its habits are also strange. It lives at the seashore and eats the seaweed that grows on rocks just below the waterline. Marine iguanas are strong swimmers and can dive almost 50 feet (15 m) below the surface. They can spend up to an hour underwater, feeding on seaweed.

The smallest reptiles are GECKOS. Some geckos don't grow longer than 1 inch (2.5 cm).

WHAT MAKES

To qualify as a reptile, an animal needs a cold-blooded body covered with dry, scaly skin. A reptile must not get too cold or too hot. To warm up, it basks in the sun. To cool down, it can crawl into the shade or take a refreshing swim.

▼ Desert lover

A chameleon is a type of reptile. We usually think of chameleons living in rain forests. But desert chameleons live in the hot, dry deserts of southern Africa. They have long, sticky tongues. They hunt insects and small reptiles among the rocks and dunes. Chameleons use their ability to change color to help control their body temperature. In the morning, a chameleon's skin is darker to absorb more heat from the sun. Toward midday, as the sun gets hotter, the chameleon changes to a pale yellow color to reflect heat away from its body.

A REPTILE?

Many reptiles SHED their SKIN several times a year. As the skin wears out, a new layer of SCALES grows beneath.

Scaly skin ▲

All reptiles have scaly skin, made from a substance called keratin. Their skin is dry and waterproof. This prevents them from losing water from their bodies. In fact, some reptiles can survive for a long time without water, which is why deserts and dry areas make ideal homes for them.

◀ Amazing feet

Reptiles are great climbers. Some lizards, such as geckos, have millions of tiny, hooklike hairs on the bottoms of their feet. These hairs allow the geckos to climb up walls and even hang upside down from ceilings.

BEWARE OF

When people think of a dragon, they imagine a huge, lizardlike beast spitting fire from its mouth. Dragons are the stuff of legend—or are they? On some remote islands in Indonesia, a giant lizard, the Komodo dragon, has the same name as the mythical creature.

▲ Deadly spit

Komodo dragons can reach 10 feet (3 m) in length and weigh more than 300 pounds (136 kg). These dragons don't breathe fire, but their saliva is full of bacteria, and it is deadly. If an animal is bitten, it usually dies within one day.

◄ Eating frenzy

Komodo dragons aren't picky eaters. They feed on deer, pigs, smaller Komodo dragons, water buffalo, and, on rare occasions, humans! During a single kill, a Komodo dragon can eat 80 percent of its own body weight.

THE DRAGON

▼ Perfect predator

The Komodo dragon hides and waits for its prey. When an animal passes by, the dragon pounces, using its powerful legs and sharp claws to overpower its victim. The dragon's serrated teeth are similar to those of a shark. It uses them to tear open the prey's skin. Then the dragon's deadly saliva seeps into its victim. The bacteria stop the blood from clotting, so the animal bleeds to death.

Komodo dragons are an ENDANGERED species because they have been hunted by humans.

HARD SHELL

People often think of turtles as slow-moving lettuce munchers. But this group of reptiles contains some truly amazing animals. The Chelonia order includes turtles, such as tortoises and terrapins.

▼ Tortoise or turtle?

All members of the Chelonia order have a shell. This is part of the animal's skeleton, and it is usually very hard and protective. Some species can draw their heads, tails, and legs inside the shell for extra protection. In general, turtles can live on both land and water. Tortoises are a kind of turtle that can live only on land. Terrapins are turtles that live only in water. Many different kinds of aquatic turtle are found in rivers, ponds, and swamps. All aquatic turtles have to come up to the surface to breathe. They have long, flexible necks that allow them to breathe more easily while the rest of their bodies remain underwater.

Flippers ▶

Loggerhead turtles are graceful swimmers and spend most of their lives in the water. They come on land only to lay their eggs. These sea turtles have large flippers instead of legs to help them move through the water.

◀ Gentle giant

Giant tortoises can measure up to 5 feet (1.5 m) from head to tail. They can also live up to 150 years! Some kinds of giant tortoise, such as the saddle-backed tortoise, have arched shells. This means the tortoise can stretch its long neck up high to reach tender shoots and leaves.

REMARKABLE

R eptiles are the oldest group of animals on Earth. In fact, they have been on the planet for more than 200 million years. Today we know more about reptiles than ever before, and many interesting facts about these creatures and their lives have come to light.

▼ Leafy tail

The leaf-tailed gecko lives only on the island of Madagascar. It is a master of disguise. As its name suggests, the tail of this gecko looks like a leaf. The rest of its body is speckled and fringed. When it lies flat against a tree branch, it is really hard to spot. Geckos are mostly nocturnal; they have huge eyes to help them see their prey at night.

The tails of some LIZARDS snap off when they are caught, which means the lizard can escape. A replacement tail soon grows!

REPTILES

◀ Ancient lizard

The tuatara lizard of New Zealand is the most ancient of all living reptiles. It's known as a living fossil because it is closely related to a group of reptiles that lived at the same time as the dinosaurs. Tuataras live to be up to 250 years old. They develop so slowly that they don't stop growing until they reach age 30.

Color sensitive ▶

Certain reptiles have developed some truly amazing colors! Red-headed agamas are medium-sized lizards that live in dry areas of Africa. Their skin changes color depending on the time of day. At night, when it's cooler, the male's body is a dark brown color. As the temperature rises during the day, the agama's color changes to blue and red-orange around its head. For this reason, these lizards are also named rainbow agamas.

FRILLS AND

With so many different kinds of reptile, it should come as no surprise that some of them look a little strange. Sometimes their behavior is pretty weird, too!

▼ Bug-eyed beast

The chameleon is a remarkable lizard. Not only are its eyes enormous, but they can also move in opposite directions from each other! This means it can see in two directions at once. A chameleon's tongue is as long as its body is, and the tip of it is sticky. When the chameleon spots a tasty meal, such as a juicy insect, it shoots out its tongue and catches the insect on the tip.

▲ Water wonder

A basilisk lizard can escape danger by running across water. Its feet are large and specially designed to keep it from sinking. This incredible behavior has earned it the nickname "Jesus Christ lizard."

SPILLS

▼ Frilling display

An Australian frilled lizard has an unusual way of defending itself. When threatened, other reptiles may play dead or run away. Not this lizard. It opens its mouth and hisses at the enemy. Then a large frill of skin expands like a huge collar around its neck. This makes the lizard seem larger and scares its enemy away.

Some HORNED LIZARDS can squirt blood out of their eyes to frighten enemies!

REPTILES

ow that you've slithered with snakes and met some other pretty freaky reptiles, you may think you know it all. Well, here are some reptile facts that might surprise you.

The largest crocodiles are SALTWATER crocodiles. They can grow to over 19 feet (6 m) long.

▲ Proud parent

Unlike many reptiles, crocodiles make great parents. When baby crocodiles hatch, the female cares for them and even carries them in her mouth, one by one, from the nest to the water's edge!

Every year in the United States, over 7,000 people are bitten by venomous snakes.

RULE!

Spiny lizard ▶

The Grand Cayman iguana can grow up to 5 feet (1.5 m) in length. Spines run along its back from neck to tail.

▼ Beady eyes

Never get into a staring contest with a snake! Snakes can't blink. They have transparent eyelids that are always closed.

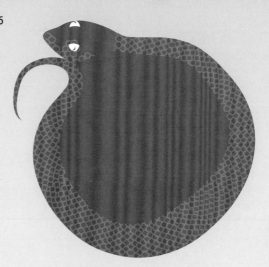

ARCTURUS CREDITS
Author: Samantha Hilton
Editor: Kate Overy
Designer: Tania Rösler
Illustrator (glasses): Ian Thompson

PICTURE CREDITS
Corbis: back cover right, p. 10 top, p. 17 top
 and bottom, p. 22 bottom, p. 27 top
Nature Picture Library: p. 7 bottom, p. 10
 bottom, p. 15 top and bottom
NHPA: title page, p. 2, p. 5 top, p. 6, p. 7 top,
 p. 8, p. 9 top and bottom, p. 11, p. 12,
 p. 13 top and bottom, p. 14, p. 19, p. 21
 top, p. 22 top, p. 23, p. 25 bottom, p. 26,
 p. 28 top and bottom, p. 30, p. 31 bottom

Oxford Scientific (OSF)/Photolibrary: p. 3 top,
 p. 5 bottom, p. 18 top, p. 20, p. 25 top,
 p. 29
Science Photo Library: p. 4, p. 16
Shutterstock: front cover, back cover left,
 p. 3 bottom, p. 18 bottom, p. 21 bottom,
 p. 24, p. 27 bottom, p. 31 top

3-D images produced by Pinsharp